A CENTURY OF READING

101 BOOKS
101 AUTHORS
THE BEST 101 BOOKS

Michael Towle

Grosvenor House
Publishing Limited

30131 05768761 5

LONDON BOROUGH OF BARNET

This book is published by
Grosvenor House Publishing Ltd
Link House
140 The Broadway, Tolworth, Surrey, KT6 7HT.
www.grosvenorhousepublishing.co.uk

A CIP record for this book
is available from the British Library

ISBN 978-1-83975-783-9

Contents

A Century of Reading

The title of The Buggles' 1979 hit, "Video Killed the Radio Star" has been used by commentators on popular culture to suggest that each form of entertainment or cerebral leisure activity has a limited lifespan before being replaced by something similar, but technologically more advanced.

One hundred years on from the world of James Joyce, EM Forster and F Scott Fitzgerald, reading is as popular as ever. A massive surprise and a massive statement, you may think, but there is the evidence to support it.

Any internet search of "the best-selling books of all time" is dominated by novels printed within the last twenty-five years. Indeed, most lists will have JK Rowling occupying at least six places in the top ten. Moving from authors to genres, we can see quite clearly that fantasy dominates, with the works of CS Lewis and JRR Tolkien being pre-eminent.

The linking of film or TV to novels may go a long way to explaining the success of certain writers, but this is nothing new. A cursory look at the highest grossing films of all time (adjusted for inflation) still has "Gone with the Wind" at the top of the list. A weighty novel if ever there was one!

What has never diminished is people's desire to be told a good story, so when we have time on our hands, what books should we read? This list may seek to recognise the classics, highlight recurring themes and celebrate popular genres, but it also strives to include variety.

While we treat some of our favourite books and authors like old friends, we should also be open to experimentation and reading something that is unfamiliar to us. These new works need to be embraced; they are not strangers. They are just friends that we have not yet made!

With these sentiments in mind, no author appears more than once on the list. There is an entry for every year and each decade has a selected book designed to capture the spirit of that particular age. This is how we have arrived at "101 Years, 101 Authors – The Best 101 Books."

The 1920s

Do we ever learn? Parallels between the 1920s and the present day make for uncanny and uncomfortable reading. A study of the decade that saw the culmination of the Spanish Flu pandemic, increasing inequalities of wealth and the struggle for women's voices to be heard, forces us to evaluate the lessons of history. Humanity was at the crossroads, just as it is now, but what was being written and read in the 1920s?

With cinema still in its adolescence and radio only in its infancy, reading was still a pastime that ordinary people relied upon to help inform their world view. So, while the infant BBC sought to "inform, educate and entertain", F Scott Fitzgerald portrayed the excesses of the super-rich, Virginia Woolf explored a feminist "stream of consciousness" and Ford Madox Ford explored a world that seemed to be descending into anarchy.

The 1920s: Book of the Decade

The Great Gatsby by F Scott Fitzgerald (1925)

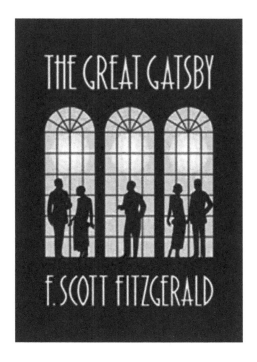

Set in the Jazz Age of 1920s New York, Fitzgerald's much acclaimed novel tells the tragic story of the millionaire Jay Gatsby and his pursuit of the beautiful, but unobtainable, Daisy Buchanan. Often viewed as one of the greatest American novels of all time, "The Great Gatsby", introduces the reader to the excessive behaviour of the excessively rich and in doing so, examines a world of which Fitzgerald was a part.

As a social commentator, Fitzgerald is extremely observant in the way that he condemns the world around him. In a period of rapid economic growth, the characters that we encounter appear to be oblivious to the dangers that lie ahead. Although Fitzgerald could not have predicted the Wall Street Crash of

1929, the reader can easily anticipate that Gatsby and his circle of friends and acquaintances are heading for disaster. It is more than coincidental that Fitzgerald's novel that preceded "The Great Gatsby" was entitled "The Beautiful and Damned". In this outwardly glamorous world, that is exactly what his characters are.

The futility and superficiality encountered in the fictional village of West Egg is narrated by Nick Carraway, who having encountered a glittering world of mansions and parties, leaves the scene at the end of the novel, returning to the Midwest. Reflecting that not only Gatsby's dreams are dead, but also that the American dream has been consumed by the mere pursuit of wealth, the narrator's disillusionment mirrors America's general disenchantment with the decade.

The 1920s: Books of the Year

1920 *The Age of Innocence* by Edith Wharton

Edith Wharton's tale of an unhappy marriage savages the snobberies of 1870s New York society. "The Age of Innocence", while painting a vivid picture of this sumptuous period, explores the love triangle involving Newland Archer, May Welland and the exciting and sophisticated Countess Olenska.

Wharton tackles universal questions related to both the head and the heart. Is love more important than wealth or future prospects? Is it possible to truly love someone without feeling the constraints of family loyalty or expectation? Set within a society that dreaded scandal above anything else, Newland Archer has some important decisions to make.

1921   *Three Soldiers* by John Dos Passos

A devastating novel that is as much a denouncement of the fate suffered by World War I soldiers as anything penned by the celebrated war poets of England, "Three Soldiers" introduces a Harvard graduate, John Andrews, to the realities of modern warfare.

With the memories of army life still very fresh in his mind, Dos Passos uses his experiences as an ambulance driver to portray the lives of a diverse trio of men drawn from completely different social and educational backgrounds. All three men are "lost in the machine" as the writer explores the brutal and dehumanising effects of a regimented war machine on ordinary men.

1922 *Ulysses* by James Joyce

Joyce's modernist tome captures a single day, June 16th 1904, in the life of the wandering Leopold Bloom and the people that he encounters. For many literary people, "Ulysses" is the most important novel of the decade and for some, the most influential work of the twentieth century.

However, "Ulysses", despite its great critical acclaim, intimidates the reader for a whole variety of reasons, including its sheer size. This accounts for it merely being the book of the year, rather than the book of the decade. Despite this, Joyce's supporters hail it as a masterpiece of wonderful extremes with its humour, sorrow and suspense.

1923 *Riceyman Steps* by Arnold Bennett

Arnold Bennett's powerful story, set just after World War I, will surprise fans of his "Five Towns" work. Gone are the nostalgically noble depictions of Bennett's working people. Instead, "Riceyman Steps" deals with the miserly life of a book dealer living in a squalid and brutalised society that has echoes of Dickensian London.

The novel is essentially a commentary of the negative effects of money as the mean-spirited Henry Earlforward refuses to spend money on his shop or home, while possessing a wardrobe full of unworn clothes. Living in a downtrodden area of London, the characters are equally downtrodden, but in Henry's case this is through his own obsessive choice.

1924 *A Passage to India* by EM Forster

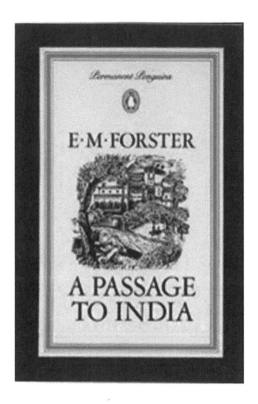

Set against a background of British imperialism and growing Indian resistance, "A Passage to India" is a triumphant novel which remains Forster's magnum opus. When Adela Quested arrives in India, her encounter with the charming and respected Dr Aziz in the Marabar caves sparks a conflict that rocks the uneasy relationship between the ruling British class and its colonial subjects.

Written at a time when the end of colonial rule in India was looking increasingly possible, this novel is much more than an attack on imperialism. It is a study of human interactions across cultures, but such friendships are doomed to failure as the light fades on "The Empire on which the sun never sets".

1925   *The Great Gatsby* by F Scott Fitzgerald
(see Book of the Decade)

1926   *The Sun Also Rises* by Ernest Hemingway

Hemingway's most accomplished novel tracks a group of young British and Americans travelling across Europe. As part of the "Lost Generation", this disillusioned group suffer from the cynicism and angst felt by many young people that survived the ravages of World War I. The characters may have survived the war, but none are unaffected by it, particularly the narrator, Jake Barnes.

The disillusioned Jake and the effervescent Lady Brett Ashley journey from the wildly decadent Paris to the bullfighting rings of Spain, accompanied by their equally disillusioned compatriots. Wandering from bar to bar, without a sense of purpose and morality, they truly are a "Lost Generation".

1927 *To the Lighthouse* by Virginia Woolf

Virginia Woolf's most innovative and pioneering novel centres on the Ramsay family's visits to the Isle of Skye. As a seminal text in the modernist tradition, "To the Lighthouse" focuses more on introspection and a stream of consciousness than any notable action. By allowing themes and ideas to take precedence over characterisation, Woolf is able to explore childhood emotions and highlight a mother's concern for the future.

The story revolves around the unimportant postponement of a family visit to a nearby lighthouse. Will the family or their friends ever go to the lighthouse? More than being a physical and highly visible object, the lighthouse symbolises a journey through life. We are always travelling "To the Lighthouse"; we are not "at" the lighthouse.

1928   *Last Post* by Ford Madox Ford

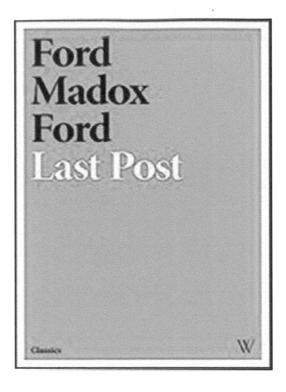

"Last Post" is the concluding story in a sequence of novels, "Parade's End". Ford sets this final volume on a single summer's day after World War I, placing his insecure characters in an uncertain world. The certainties that once existed have now been eroded and those who experienced the war have returned to a world that appears to be descending into anarchy.

The joy of the armistice may have been replaced by disillusionment. The English ancestral home may have been let to an American and its great tree felled, but England and its people do have a future. A new beginning awaits Christopher and Valentine, albeit an uncertain one.

1929 *The Sound and the Fury* by William Faulkner

A novel taking its title from Macbeth's observation that life is "a tale told by an idiot, full of sound and fury, signifying nothing", Faulkner's work both enlightens and confuses the reader. Over a thirty-year period, that is narrated from four different perspectives, the Compson family sees its wealth and status disappear. The first section is narrated by Benjy, the mentally retarded youngest son of an alcoholic father and a hypochondriac mother. Not a promising start!

The Compsons, like the Macbeths, are portrayed as a family whose wounds can never heal. With its unconventional structure, "The Sound and the Fury" details the decline and tragedy of a prestigious Mississippi family in devastating fashion.

The 1930s

If the previous decade had been one of disappointment and disillusionment, what defined the history and writing of the 1930s? While much of the literature of the Great Depression was severe in its social criticism, some writers viewed the decade as an opportunity to reflect on earlier, but no less traumatic periods of history. While Vera Brittain's unsurpassed autobiography recalled the waste of life and the subsequent feelings of loss from the First World War, "Gone with the Wind" also required the reader to sympathise with the major characters' struggle for survival, despite their privileged backgrounds.

Disillusioned with the effects of capitalism and armed with the realisation that the American Dream was not available to all people, Steinbeck and his adherents sought to portray the contemporary poor as honest, decent people struggling to survive adversity in much the same way as the idealised, but racially ignorant, characters of "The Little House on the Prairie". 1930s literature, with its envious looking back into history, has fuelled much debate, but what is almost indisputable is that it contained very little to prepare readers for the horrors of World War Two.

The 1930s: Book of the Decade

Brave New World by Aldous Huxley (1932)

Aldous Huxley's classic dystopian novel is set in a futuristic World State which, rather disturbingly, has close parallels with the present day. Despite being published almost ninety years ago, the subject matter of "Brave New World" appears very familiar to us. Genetic engineering, a reliance upon recreational drugs and a society divided into separate social classes are topics for discussion today.

Huxley questions the morality and values of 1930s Britain, but far in the future the rulers of the World State have created a utopia where all members of a brainwashed society are happy. We soon realise, however, that the psychological control exerted over people has created a dystopian existence that is only challenged by one person: the protagonist, Bernard Marx. Although set approximately six hundred years in the future, "Brave New World" is very much a novel of its time. The 1930s was a period of great political and economic change and Huxley captured the concerns of that period to create a world in which all the anxieties about the future became a frightening reality.

The emergence of socialism, in Huxley's hands, becomes a totalitarian World State. The inter-war years saw a gradual weakening of the hold that conventional religion had over people and the growth of materialistic attitudes in the west. "Brave New World" transforms these ideas into a religion of consumerism that sees Henry Ford as a deity. As all the identical cars roll off the assembly line, will humans also be mass-produced in the future?

X No mention of title alluding to/from Shakespeare's X "The Tempest".

The 1930s: Books of the Year

1930   *The Maltese Falcon* by Dashiell Hammett

Hammett's detective novel places Sam Spade, the detached and occasionally ruthless detective, in a dangerous world where he can become both the hunter and the hunted. He is the determined, experienced detective who plays by his own set of rules in his pursuit of the jewel encrusted falcon, but is the beautiful Brigid O'Shaughnessy to be trusted?

The detached third person narrative, where the characters' thoughts, feelings and emotions are eradicated, means that the reader only sees physical actions and descriptions. Within this framework, Sam Spade's cold heart and keen eye for detail make him the ideal detective for the Hollywood treatment that he gets when acted by the incomparable Humphrey Bogart.

1931   *The Five Red Herrings* by Dorothy L Sayers

In this, the seventh novel in the Lord Peter Wimsey series, Dorothy L Sayers gives the resolutely fearless detective yet another case to solve, but while trying to investigate the suspicious death of an artist, he finds that all the major suspects keep disappearing. What makes the case even more difficult to solve for the intrepid hero is that nobody appears sorry to see the demise of the Scottish painter.

The detective is not helped by the character of the victim. Who would mourn a man that was an obnoxious drunkard that seemed to quarrel with everybody who was unfortunate enough to cross his path? There are several people in this artistic commune that detested him, but who would detest him enough to kill him?

1932   *Brave New World* by Aldous Huxley
       (See Book of the Decade)

1933   *Testament of Youth* by Vera Brittain

Vera Brittain's outstanding memoirs is a brilliant depiction of the impact that World War I had upon the lives of women and the aspiring middle-classes of England. Having lost her brother, her fiancé and several friends in the war, Brittain recalls all that she has lived through as she mourns a vanished generation. Her struggles are compounded by the resistance of a conservative society that feels threatened by educated women.

Nearly a century on, "Testament of Youth" remains probably the most powerful and compelling war memoirs of all time. Being both a pacifist and a feminist, Brittain's work and reputation has tended to slip in and out of popularity, but what needs to be celebrated is that "Testament of Youth" is beautifully and movingly written.

1934   *I, Claudius* by Robert Graves

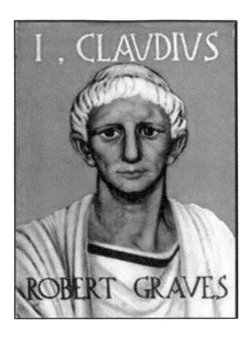

Robert Graves' historical novel is written in the form of an autobiography by the Roman Emperor Claudius. Although the narrative is fiction, the events are drawn from reputable historical accounts. The stammering Claudius has to face all the political intrigue, cruelty and depravity that the Roman Empire can throw at him, and in so doing earns the reader's unbounded sympathy and respect.

Said to be historical fiction of the highest order, "I, Claudius" covers almost every human action that is violent or immoral though the eyes of a man disregarded by both his family and his peers. Being regarded as inconsequential, Claudius is left alone to record a remarkable tale and a riveting read.

1935 *Little House on the Prairie* by Laura Ingalls Wilder

Laura Ingalls Wilder's autobiographical children's novel is part of the "Little House" series and charts her travels across the prairie to Kansas where her father builds the small family home. Life in 1870s pioneering country is hard, occasionally dangerous, but Laura and her family settle happily into their new home until conflict catches up with them.

In addition to suffering from malaria and seeing its crops fail on several occasions, the family is at the forefront of the dispute over Indian lands. Life that was once difficult and uncertain, now becomes precarious. Will the American dream have to be fulfilled somewhere else?

1936 *Gone with the Wind* by Margaret Mitchell

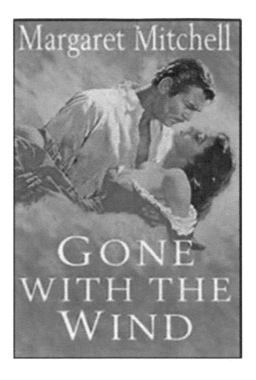

Although more famous as a film, "Gone with the Wind" is a giant of a novel within the canon of American literature. Set in the American Civil War, Scarlett O'Hara is forced to use all of her immense resourcefulness to overcome the realities of poverty, violence and slavery. Despite the heartbreak and disasters that she suffers, Scarlett remains one of the most unremittingly optimistic characters in 20th century literature.

Despite producing an immense amount of criticism for its portrayal of slavery and black Americans, "Gone with the Wind" is a masterpiece of characterisation. How else can we account for our admiration for a heroine that is vain, self-centred and spoilt?

1937 *The Hobbit* by JRR Tolkien

Tolkien's "The Hobbit" is a children's fantasy novel set in a fictional universe which follows the quest of Bilbo Baggins to help the dwarves reclaim their treasure from the fearsome dragon Smaug. The novel is a tale of bravery as Bilbo's adventures place him in great danger. Will he prevail over adversity and justify Gandalf's claim that there is more to the little hobbit than meets the eye?

Originally written by Tolkien for reading to his own children, "The Hobbit" is so much more than just a family favourite. This tale of unforgettable characters and fantastic adventures can be enjoyed by adults and children alike.

1938 *Rebecca* by Daphne du Maurier

"Last night I dreamt I went to Manderley again." Puzzlingly famous words, but what is the context? The opening line of "Rebecca" transports the reader into a world of deception with a complex story that is both passionate and psychologically challenging.

Narrated mostly by flashbacks, Daphne du Maurier's psychological thriller concerns an unnamed woman who becomes increasingly insecure as she recalls past events in her life. There is a hypnotic quality to this narrative that entraps and then holds the reader in an almost claustrophobic grip.

Readable and riveting, this haunting international bestseller has never been out of print, but it has only recently gained the critical acclaim that its popularity with the public deserved and had previously been denied.

1939   *The Grapes of Wrath* by John Steinbeck

Steinbeck's epic novel of the Great Depression tells the story of an unfortunate Oklahoma family who, having lost their homestead, are forced to travel to the promised land of California. The migrant life of the Joad family is a story of thwarted aspirations and broken promises.

"The Grapes of Wrath" highlights the conflict and inequalities in America between the powerful rich and the powerless poor, but out of these injustices the family unit remains largely intact. The Joad's harrowing journey sees them deal with poverty, death, bullying and exploitation. Amazingly, the dignity of poor people can survive, but the American dream is not available for all Americans!

The 1940s

While much of the literature of the inter-war period had advocated economic, social or political change, mankind was not prepared for the cataclysmic change that was unleashed after 1939. Both the literature of the period and the decade itself significantly divide into two distinct halves: pre-1945 and post-1945.

We may expect that both traditional and popular culture would flounder or become morbid in the midst of international conflict and "total war", but this was not the case. Wartime saw the flowering of British cinema's "Golden Age" and books came to symbolise freedom. Only when the war ended did writers truly reflect upon their traumatic experiences and their negative view of a future world. The diary of Ann Frank and Szpilman's "The Pianist" told stories of how the human spirit finds ways to exist in extreme circumstances, but they were the precursors of "Nineteen Eighty-Four".

The most optimistic book in the list is written by Betty Smith, whose tree not only "Grows in Brooklyn", but survives and flourishes. Not everyone was forced to move from old war to Cold War.

The 1940s: Book of the Decade

Nineteen Eighty-Four by George Orwell (1949)

The impact and importance of "Nineteen Eighty-Four" is difficult to exaggerate. Orwell's chilling dystopian novel acts as a warning against the inevitable excesses of totalitarianism. Simultaneous to the Berlin Airlift, when the Soviet blockade threatened the very existence of people living in the western half of this divided city, Orwell's greatest work attacks the excesses of politically extreme regimes.

Feeding on the western fear of communism, "Nineteen Eighty-Four" has become a byword for omnipresent government surveillance. The phrases and ideas used by Orwell have found their way into mainstream culture and vocabulary in a way that the words of many other authors have not. How often have we heard that "Big Brother" is watching us? Have our frustrations with modern political correctness led us to accuse our critics as belonging to the "Thought Police"? To take the analogy further, when we don't trust our government and its institutions, we are prone to use the adjective "Orwellian" and then consign anything that we don't like to "Room 101". Not since Shakespeare has a writer had such a profound influence on the English language and its usage as George Orwell.

With all its political, sociological and linguistic importance, it needs to be remembered that "Nineteen Eighty-Four" is also a brilliantly written and compellingly tense thriller. We follow the story of the rebellious protagonist, Winston Smith, who works in the Records Department of the Ministry of Truth, where his job is to rewrite historical documents to match the party line. This is the story of one man, but the commonality of his surname means that it could be the story of every man.

The 1940s: Books of the Year

1940 *The Heart Is a Lonely Hunter* by Carson McCullers

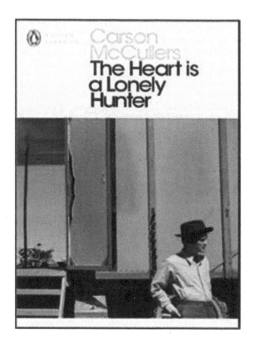

The debut novel of Carson McCullers pitches its protagonist, the deaf John Singer, into a world of loneliness and isolation. How will Singer cope when his mute companion of ten years is placed in an asylum? Who will "speak" to him? As it turns out, nearly all the social misfits of the town confide in him.

At surface level, "The Heart Is a Lonely Hunter" is primarily about the daily struggles of an incongruous group of lonely and dispossessed characters in 1930s Georgia. However, at a deeper level, McCullers is tackling huge issues in American society, such as racial inequality and grinding poverty, with great insight and power.

1941 *The Keys of the Kingdom* by AJ Cronin

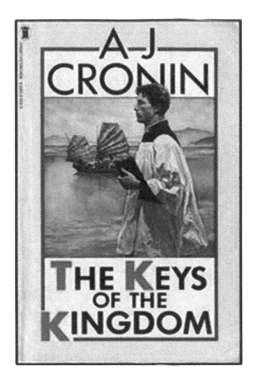

Cronin's protagonist, Father Francis Chisholm, finds the tragedies of his youth replaced by the hardships, dangers and poverty of missionary work in China. Against this background, can a devout and humble man find "The Keys of the Kingdom" and attain eternal life? What becomes of a good man called to do good in a cruel world?

Chisholm is a compassionate man, but he is both disliked and considered a failure by his superiors. He is, however, a success when we measure his level of holiness against that of other clergymen. This is because he has asked God to judge him more by his intentions than his actual deeds. His salvation lies in the fact that his intentions have always been honourable.

1942 *The Stranger* by Albert Camus

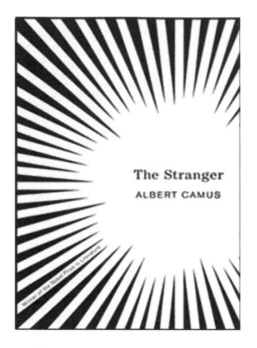

"Mother died today. Or maybe it was yesterday, I don't know." Albert Camus' story is that of an ordinary man whose behaviour is far from ordinary. Meursault receives the news of his mother's death with extraordinary detachment. His lack of emotion may alarm those around him, but not as much as some of his later behaviour alarms the reader.

Meursault's philosophy is that of the absurd and his detached nature governs his actions and attitudes throughout the novel. Through his major character, Camus appears to assert that both individual lives and society's expectations have no rational order or meaning. The absurdity expressed in the novel suggests that any attempt to find such order or meaning, where none exists, is futile.

1943 *A Tree Grows in Brooklyn* by Betty Smith

Betty Smith's debut novel is a semi-autobiographical tale of an immigrant family in early 20th century Brooklyn, New York. Despite the deprivation and poverty, the remarkable Nolan family make it possible for Francie, their eldest daughter, to follow her aspirations. The tree in the book's title that survives and flourishes in the harsh urban environment mirrors the indefatigable heroine's quest to grow and prosper.

"A Tree Grows in Brooklyn" is a consummate novel. Beautifully written, it elicits every emotion in the sensitive reader. There is immense sadness, but at its heart this book is about the triumph of hope and determination over adversity. We identify with Betty Smith's story because we sympathise with the flawed characters who invariably try to do what is right.

1944 *The Razor's Edge* by W Somerset Maugham

"The Razor's Edge" details the change in personality suffered by Larry Darrell, an American pilot traumatised by his experiences in World War I. His rejection of his pre-war values leads him, after some elaborate preparations, to search for a true spiritual meaning to life, but will his time spent in India provide all the answers to his questions?

Essentially, "The Razor's Edge" is the journey of a young man trying to find enlightenment as he chooses an alternative path to that trodden by most of his more socially conventional contemporaries. Spirituality eventually triumphs over materialism and Larry is one of the few characters that finds true happiness and fulfilment.

1945   *The Berlin Novels* by Christopher Isherwood

"The Berlin Novels" is a book consisting of two astonishingly related works by Christopher Isherwood: "Mr Norris Changes Trains" and "Goodbye to Berlin". Isherwood magnificently captures 1931 Berlin, with its charms, dangers and debaucheries in equal measure. The creation of characters is equally stunning, with the misadventures of the unforgettable Sally Bowles later being popularised on the cinema screen by Liza Minelli in "Cabaret".

Isherwood's great strength as a writer lies in his engagingly vivid portrayal of both people and places. His characters may be morally degenerate, but they are still endearing. Our concerns for them are palpable as they act out their story on the stage of a politically chaotic and frightening Berlin.

1946 *The Pianist* by Władysław Szpilman

"The Pianist" is a memoir by the Polish-Jewish pianist and composer Władysław Szpilman in which he describes his life in German occupied Poland during World War II. After being forced to live in the Warsaw Ghetto, Szpilman manages to avoid deportation to the Nazi death camps and survives in the ruined city with the help of friends and strangers, including a German officer who admires his piano playing.

Many people have turned to the novel after watching Roman Polanski's excellent 2002 film of the same name. Almost without exception, they have not been disappointed. Although a relatively short book, "The Pianist" brings the horror and brutality of Nazi rule to life. The enduring emotions, however, are those of admiration and amazement at one man's capacity for survival.

1947   *The Diary of a Young Girl* by Anne Frank

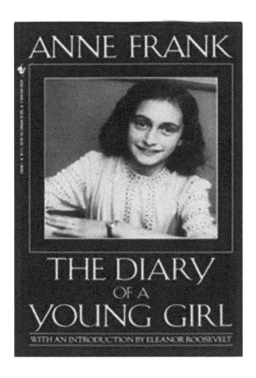

Only after the end of World War II did the true extent of Nazi atrocities come to light. Following on from "The Pianist", we encounter another beautifully crafted story of the struggle to both hide and survive in German occupied Europe.

Commonly known as "The Diary of Anne Frank", this remarkable book has become a world classic. In 1942, with the Nazis occupying Holland, a young Jewish girl and her family fled their home in Amsterdam and went into hiding. In her diary Anne Frank recorded vivid impressions of her experiences during the two years before her betrayal to the Gestapo. Anne Frank's account is a profoundly moving story, one about the experiences of an ordinary teenage girl living in extraordinary circumstances.

1948 *The Heart of the Matter* by Graham Greene

Set in a small colonial outpost in West Africa during World War II, "The Heart of the Matter" details a life-changing crisis of morality for the enigmatic police officer, Henry Scobie. Powerful and thought provoking, "The Heart of the Matter" draws upon the author's experience of working for the Foreign Office in Sierra Leone. Scobie is torn between compassion for his wife, with whom he shares a loveless marriage, and pity for a young widow that he has an affair with. His sense of shame and guilt leads him to contemplate suicide.

At its core, Greene's work is a novel of moral dilemmas. Is it possible to make other people happy? Can suicide ever be justified?

1949 *Nineteen Eighty-Four* by George Orwell
   (See Book of the Decade)

The 1950s

Were the 1950s an era of fulfilled hope and optimism or one of stagnation? The 1951 Festival of Britain and the hopes expressed for a new "Elizabethan Age" suggested that an exciting future lay ahead. America's emergence as a democratic, political and economic superpower gave wealth and financial freedom to more of its inhabitants than ever before.

Critics of the 1950s tend to view the decade as one of complacency and missed opportunity. However, the decade in which the British Prime Minister Harold Macmillan stated that, "You've never had it so good," forged an opposition to the status quo that believed quite the reverse. Dystopian literature abounded and William Golding's seminal work, "Lord of the Flies", gave power to the notion that man left to his own devices will ultimately destroy.

The fears of the Cold War sat uneasily alongside condemnation of colonialism, but was it really a decade, to quote Chinua Achebe, in which "Things Fall Apart"? The "Angry Young Men" of the new British drama and the writers of America's "Beat Generation" may have attacked Britain's class structure and the economic materialism of respectable America, but the world of "Peyton Place" survived.

The 1950s: Book of the Decade

Things Fall Apart by Chinua Achebe (1958)

"Things Fall Apart" details the tragic life of Okonkwo, a young Igbo man who finds fame in his area of Nigeria as a wrestling champion. The novel tells how his strength makes him one of the most powerful men of his clan. In this archetypal African novel, Okonkwo builds his life along extremely masculine lines by working on the land, taking wives and producing numerous children to carry on his name and reputation. He is the product of a people that respects strength, loyalty and a strict adherence to traditional values.

However, the backdrop to his story is a changing world brought about by colonialism and zealous Christian missionary work. Missionaries come to Okonkwo's village, bringing with them a culture that is alien to him. Achebe, in presenting this juxtaposition of cultures, seeks to educate a western audience about the Igbo customs and proverbs and, consequently, the value of traditional African life.

Compared to a lot of post-colonial writing, Achebe's novel is relatively even-handed. The conflict between tradition and change is not merely a binary choice. Change is deemed to be necessary, but traditional cultures should not be consumed by the arrival of westernised ideas. Equally important is an individual's fear of losing his status within his own people. Okonkwo's downturn in fortunes is the reverse of the lowly clan-members, whose adoption of a Christian way of life sees them elevated to a level previously unknown or impossible within such an ancient hierarchical society.

The 1950s: Books of the Year

1950 *The Lion, the Witch and the Wardrobe* by CS Lewis

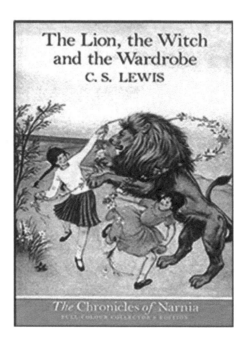

The best known of the seven novels in "The Chronicles of Narnia", "The Lion, the Witch and the Wardrobe" is both a fantasy and a fantastic book for children. The novel has the great advantage of being an enchanting read in its own right or as part of a fabulous collection.

The majority of the story is set in Narnia; a mythical land beyond the wardrobe door and a secret place frozen in eternal winter. This is a magical country waiting to be set free from the White Witch's sinister spell. This second book in CS Lewis' classic fantasy series has enthralled readers of all ages since its first publication, drawing them into an entrancing world inhabited by unforgettable characters.

1951 *The Catcher in the Rye* by JD Salinger

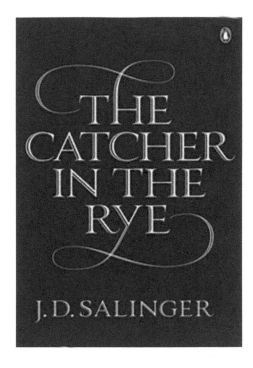

JD Salinger's classic coming-of-age novel details the three days following Holden Caulfield's expulsion from his latest exclusive and expensive boarding school just before the Christmas holiday. What can a sixteen-year-old boy do to avoid returning home suspiciously early?

With what money he possesses, Holden decides to explore New York for a few days. His journey of self-discovery and the search for truth leads him into some dangerous and debauched situations. As Holden is exposed to some of the worst excesses that America's largest city has to offer, Salinger takes the loss of innocence as his primary theme. Holden wants to be "The Catcher in the Rye": the person who saves children from falling off a metaphorical cliff.

1952 *Invisible Man* by Ralph Ellison

"Invisible Man" addresses many of the social, political and intellectual issues faced by black Americans in the early twentieth century. The unnamed narrator begins his story by claiming that he is an "invisible man." His interpretation of invisibility is that when members of the dominant white society see him, they view him as a collection of racial stereotypes rather than as an actual person. Not only do people fail to see him, but they refuse to see him.

On his frightening journey from America's Deep South to the streets of New York, Ellison's nameless protagonist tells a story that goes way beyond the experiences of one individual and gives a voice to all those opposed to the bigotry of post-war America.

1953 *Fahrenheit 451* by Ray Bradbury

Ray Bradbury's dystopian novel presents a view of a future American society where books are outlawed and any that are found are burnt. The title, "Fahrenheit 451", refers to the temperature at which books catch fire. The novel has inevitably sparked debate on the historical significance of burning books, with all its overtones of suppressing any ideas that may run contrary to the dominant political or philosophical ideology of the time.

Additionally, it is a comment on an era when television and the media gained greater importance at the expense of reading. The protagonist, Guy Montag, is a fireman who becomes disillusioned with his job of censoring books and destroying knowledge. Eventually, Guy quits his job and commits himself to the preservation of literature and cultural writing.

1954 *Lord of the Flies* by William Golding

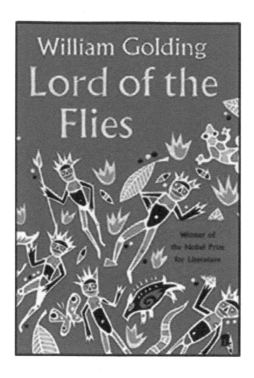

Yet another dystopian novel joins the list in the years following World War II. "Lord of the Flies" is one of the most memorable novels about "the end of innocence" and "the darkness of man's heart."

The novel focuses on a group of British boys stranded on an uninhabited island and their disastrous attempt to govern themselves. As the boys divide into two factions and the level of violence and destruction increases, we are led to the apocalyptic view that mankind left to his own devices will inevitably destroy life. Looking to our own future, perhaps this novel should be declared to be compulsory reading for all young people.

1955 *Lolita* by Vladimir Nabokov

Pushing the boundaries of literary acceptability, Nabokov's controversial novel is notable for its problematic subject matter and the reactions that it has generated. How are lovers of literature meant to react? The novel is beautifully written, but reading about a middle-aged literature professor, falling completely and hopelessly in love with the twelve-year-old Lolita, is disturbing.

However, "Lolita" is extraordinarily powerful, challenging us to read beyond our disgust and to live inside the mind of Humbert. This complex character has evoked numerous and contradictory reactions. Is he genuinely in love or just insane? Does he have a soul to be pitied or merely despised? The truth may be a combination of all these interpretations.

1956 *Peyton Place* by Grace Metalious

"Peyton Place" uncovers the passions and deceits that simmer beneath the surface of an outwardly perfect New England town. Each of the three women at the centre of the story have a secret to hide and each of them is forced to come to terms with their own identity against a background of hypocrisy, adultery and even murder.

Such was the popularity of the novel, and its subsequent television incarnations over the next two decades, that the term "Peyton Place" became synonymous with any small gossipy town that held scandalous secrets. The interest generated by the novel's incest, adultery and sexual tensions helped to make "Peyton Place" the "Fifty Shades of Grey" of the 1950s.

1957   *On the Road* by Jack Kerouac

"On the Road" is a brilliant blend of fiction and autobiographical experiences in which the innocent Sal Paradise joins his hero Dean Moriarty on a hedonistic search for fulfilment. Based on the travels of Kerouac and his friends across the United States, the novel is invariably viewed as the defining work of the post-war "beat" generation, with its protagonists living life against an intoxicating background of sex, jazz and drug use.

This tale of a breathless and exhilarating ride back and forth across America was apparently written in a drug induced three-week period, which may explain the frantic nature of the journey. However, for Kerouac it's the journey that matters, not the destination.

1958 *Things Fall Apart* by Chinua Achebe
      (See Book of the Decade)

1959 *Cider with Rosie* by Laurie Lee

The novel is an account of the author's blissful childhood in a Gloucestershire village, soon after World War I. It chronicles the traditional village life which disappeared with the advent of new developments such as the emergence of the motor car and the use of electricity. In relating the experiences of childhood many years later, Lee places his adoring mother, struggling to raise a family, at the centre of the action.

"Cider with Rosie" is so much more than a nostalgic look back at Laurie Lee's childhood; it is a remarkable commentary on a lost world that existed slightly less than a century ago. It opens a window into a different time and place when people owned less, but experienced more.

The 1960s

American actor and comedian Charlie Fleischer observed that: "If you remember the '60s, you really weren't there." Was it a magical age in which all the hypocrisies and accepted norms of society from previous decades were either swept away or slayed on the altar of drug-infused experimentation, free love and self-expression?

Our list of 1960s books opens with Harper Lee's "To Kill a Mocking Bird" wrestling against America's racial inequality. This, perhaps, set the scene for a decade in which the literature flowed with the turbulence of the times. What cannot be denied is that writers and producers of books, plays, music and art seized their newly won opportunities to speak to a world that was receptive to change.

More than half a century later, a balanced evaluation of this most radical of decades would suggest that the "Swinging Sixties" really did give birth to new social attitudes, greater educational opportunities and fresh ways of looking at the world. In the anti-war decade of protests against nuclear arms and the Vietnam War, two anti-war novels find their way on to our list, with the second one appearing straight after John Updike's study of 1960s promiscuity in "Couples". It's true that Bob Dylan spoke for a decade, or even a generation, with "The Times They Are a-Changin".

The 1960s: Book of the Decade

To Kill a Mockingbird by Harper Lee (1960)

Several novels on our list fall under the category of nostalgia, with writers looking back fondly to their childhood or adolescence. Now it's the turn of the reader. How many of us read this book at high school or purely for pleasure? Renowned for its humour, accessibility and warmth, "To Kill a Mockingbird" quickly became a classic of American literature. Harper Lee's novel, based upon her own observations of life in 1930s Alabama, delivers a devastating account of racial inequality and the heroic attempts of the narrator's father to seek justice against a background of bigotry and ignorance.

The film adaptation, with Gregory Peck's superb portrayal of the heroic lawyer and father, Atticus Finch, adds to the magnificence and the reputation of the novel. Such is its popularity, that our book of the decade could easily challenge for the title of "Book of the Century". Despite being one of the top selling books of all time about race, "To Kill a Mockingbird" remained Lee's only published novel until "Go Set a Watchman" in 2015.

An analysis of the novel's unusual title is built on the narrative where Atticus and Miss Maudie tell Scout and her brother Jem that, "it's a sin to kill a mockingbird." Thus, mockingbirds symbolise innocence and beauty in the novel. Atticus and Miss Maudie tell Scout and Jem because these birds cause no harm to anyone or anything. They just sing, and in doing so, they make the world a more beautiful place. As well as being a commentary on the evils and ignorance of racism, "To Kill a Mockingbird" is a classic "coming of age" novel.

The 1960s: Books of the Year

1960   *To Kill a Mockingbird* by Harper Lee

(See Book of the Decade)

1961   *Catch-22* by Joseph Heller

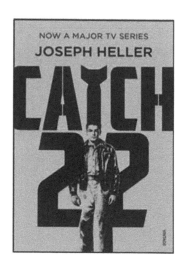

Joseph Heller's "Catch-22" is a satirical novel which details the absurdities of war. Captain John Yossarian of the U.S. Army Air Forces acts as the anti-hero stationed in Italy during World War II. Not only are the practices of warfare and military bureaucracy mocked and questioned, but Heller invites readers to challenge almost everything that is familiar to them.

This satirical novel is often credited as being one of the most significant books of the twentieth century, with its title passing into common usage within the English language. At a practical level, it reminds us of the precarious nature of life and the value that we must attach to it. So, can Yossarian and his colleagues maintain their sanity and return home safely?

1962 *A Clockwork Orange* by Anthony Burgess

"A Clockwork Orange" is a novel whose reputation precedes a serious reading of it. Of all those that have heard about it, very few have read it, perhaps being put off by its reputation for shocking violence and the feral behaviour of its youth subculture. In short, the novel is a dystopian, nightmarish vision of the future, with its teenage protagonist narrating his violent exploits and his experiences with state authorities that are intent on reforming him.

What is the true meaning of human freedom? Burgess questions the morality of free will and the desirability of societal control. At the heart of the matter is the question: is it better to choose to be bad or to be conditioned to be good?

1963 *The Bell Jar* by Sylvia Plath

Sylvia Plath's only novel is an intensely emotional account of a woman falling into the grip of insanity. "The Bell Jar" details the life of a beautiful, talented and successful woman, Esther Greenwood, as she finds herself grappling with difficult relationships and descending into serious depression. Is there an escape for her in this male dominated world or will she suffocate under a "bell jar"?

Sadly, any reader with a knowledge of Plath's own descent into clinical depression and eventual suicide will find it almost impossible to separate the heroine from the author. However, the beauty of the writing and the subtle awareness of the heroine's situation make this a very powerful and poignant read.

1964 *The Spy Who Came in from the Cold* by John Le Carré

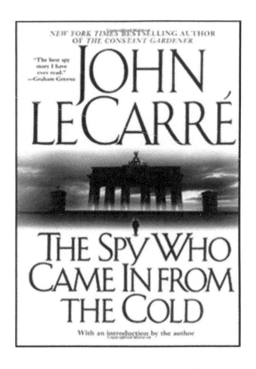

John Le Carré's Cold War spy novel introduces the reader to Alec Leamas, a senior British agent who has returned to London from Berlin from a frightening assignment. As the title suggests, Leamas is yearning to "come in from the cold", but his superiors have an extremely dangerous mission in mind for him on the other side of the Iron Curtain: to kill the head of the East German secret service.

This is a novel with a tightly woven and brilliantly executed plot. The action is rapid and a tremendous ensemble of characters, as befitting the world that they operate in, manage to blur the lines between good and evil. It appears that western espionage methods do not quite measure up to western values.

1965 *The Magus* by John Fowles

Fowles' postmodern novel is a daring literary thriller, with Nicholas Urfe, an Oxford graduate, at its centre. The young Englishman accepts a teaching position in a private boys' school on the Greek island of Phraxos, where he befriends a local millionaire. While exploring the island, Nicholas discovers a remote villa, owned by Conchis; an elderly man with enormous wealth and a mysterious background.

Their friendship soon evolves into a deadly game, in which reality and fantasy are deliberately manipulated. Nicholas soon finds himself the victim of various masquerades and is led on a journey beyond his wildest imaginings. As the narrative unfolds, he also discovers that he must fight not only for his sanity, but also for his very survival.

1966 *Wide Sargasso Sea* by Jean Rhys

Most readers are familiar with the mad woman in the attic in "Jane Eyre", but very little is known about Mr Rochester's first wife. Have we ever stopped to imagine what her side of the story is? Well, Jean Rhys has, and she tells Antoinette's story in all its dramatic colours, making "Wide Sargasso Sea" the feminist, anti-colonial response to Charlotte Brontë's story.

The Creole heiress, Antoinette, finds herself belonging to neither England nor Jamaica. She is neither black nor white and is not fully accepted by either. This is not a comfortable place for her in the post-emancipation era. As the daughter of a slave owner, Antoinette must become accustomed to change, unrest and hatred.

1967 *One Hundred Years of Solitude* by Gabriel Garcia Marquez

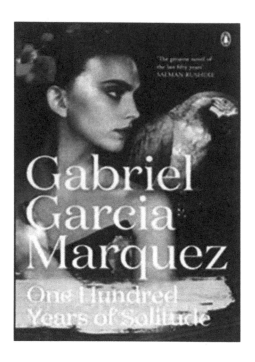

"One Hundred Years of Solitude" is considered to be the foremost example of the genre known as magical realism, but to try to confine Márquez's great masterpiece within a single genre of fiction serves only to constrain its importance and its appeal. Both a fable and a fairy tale, an epic and a chronicle, the novel is the story of seven generations of the Buendía family and the fictitious town of Macondo that they have built.

"One Hundred Years of Solitude" comfortably blends fantasy and reality, making it a compelling, but sometimes complicated read. Macondo has its share of wars, conflicts and disasters, but its secrets remain hidden in one of the twentieth century's most daring and original pieces of literature.

1968 *2001: A Space Odyssey* by Arthur C. Clarke

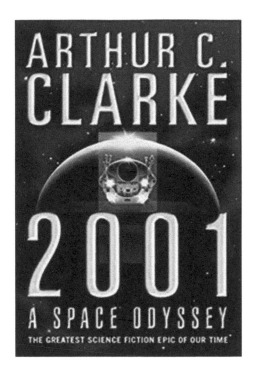

For most discerning readers, the book is always better than the film! Why is this? Partly because the book is nearly always produced first, but with "2001: A Space Odyssey" Arthur C Clarke's novel and Stanley Kubrick's film were developed concurrently, with both men feeding each other ideas.

The film is probably more famous within popular culture, but the novel is a landmark piece of science fiction writing, where Clarke cuts to humanity's need to question the universe and its constituent parts. Published the year before man walked on the moon, 2001 seemed to be in the very distant future. Such is the quality of the writing that now, twenty years on from that date, the book still seems both fresh and futuristic.

1969 *Slaughterhouse-Five* by Kurt Vonnegut

Frequently cited as a modern classic, Kurt Vonnegut's non-linear narrative details the life of Billy Pilgrim, an American prisoner of war held in Dresden towards the end of World War II. Billy manages to survive the controversial Allied firebombing of the city by hiding in the underground meat locker known as "Slaughterhouse Five".

Based upon Kurt Vonnegut's own wartime experiences, this book is much more than the ordinary stereotypical anti-war novel. Using flashbacks and elements of time travel, "Slaughterhouse Five" is an extraordinary mix of genre that provides a whole range of experiences for the reader. There is a fascinating blend of tragedy, comic relief and science fiction to be found within this one jumbled and absurd, yet fantastic, novel.

The 1970s

Following on from the transformative and revolutionary decade that proceeded it, the 1970s has suffered from a negative press not dished out with such severity to any other post-war decade. Economic decay and political unrest are the dominant images of an era that is portrayed as a long hangover from the joyous party that was the '60s. With "dodgy haircuts", and even dodgier fashions, 1970s youth faced a very uncertain future, but was this the complete picture?

In truth, most people were more prosperous than previous generations. Foreign holidays became attainable like never before and man's first walking on the Moon was still a recent and vivid memory. In a world of expanding horizons, what were people reading?

The thoughts of writers from outside of Britain and America certainly came to prominence in this decade. People in the west all had ideas about the Soviet Union. They knew that it was no socialist utopia, but they embraced the thoughts of Solzhenitsyn because he had suffered the extreme effects of tyranny. In 1978 "post-colonial literature" as a term was still nearly a decade away, but in line with the British fascination with empire, the last two books on our list deal with the antagonisms of imperial life in Africa and India. Readers were prepared to look beyond "A Bend in the River" to learn about "The Far Pavilions"!

The 1970s: Book of the Decade

A Bend in the River by VS Naipaul (1979)

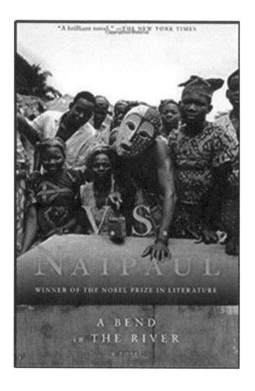

VS Naipaul's post-colonial masterpiece tells the story of Salim, a young man of Indian origin, trying to run a small business in an unnamed central African country. Having taken over a shop, deep inland by "A Bend in the River", just after independence, Salim observes the early political struggles and difficulties of his newly adopted country. Observing the waves of unrest and uncertainty, Salim virtually becomes an outsider, watching unfolding events with an outsider's nervousness. The country's President, referred to as the Big Man, initially rules the country with a relatively benign hand, but year by year and chapter by chapter the Big Man becomes increasingly more dictatorial.

Comparisons between several contemporary African countries and Naipaul's depiction of mounting chaos, declining economic fortunes and the abandonment of democratic principles have led to controversy. "A Bend in the River" is a truly moving story, but it has led to accusations that the author was an apologist for colonial rule in Africa. Is he a colonialist writing post-colonial literature? Seen as a literary heir to Joseph Conrad, whose "Heart of Darkness" was also set on an African river, it may be construed that attitudes to African self-determination have hardly moved forward in the seventy years dividing the two publications.

Leaving aside the debates and controversies, the great strength of "A Bend in the River" is that the leisurely pace of the narrative allows the characters and the setting to be introduced and then developed in detail. The subject matter is complex, but Naipaul's style is poetic and almost effortless.

The 1970s: Books of the Year

1970 *The Bluest Eye* by Toni Morrison

Set in Morrison's hometown of Lorain, Ohio, "The Bluest Eye" tells the story of an eleven-year-old black girl called Pecola Breedlove, who grows up in poverty during the years following the Great Depression.

Set in 1941, the story tells us that due to her mannerisms and dark skin, she is consistently regarded as being "ugly". As a result, she develops an inferiority complex, which fuels her desire for the blue eyes that she equates with "whiteness" and beauty. Pecola connects beauty with being loved and believes that if she possesses blue eyes, the cruelty in her life will be replaced by affection and respect. Written almost three decades after it is set, the novel reflects the increasing rejection by African Americans of racial and cultural stereotypes.

1971 *Wheels* by Arthur Hailey

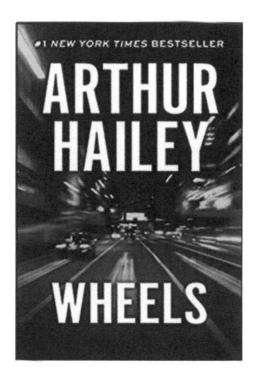

"Wheels" takes an in-depth look at the process of the development of a new car before it enters the market. The novel, however, is about a lot more than just cars: it is also about the lives of the people working in the motor industry. Detroit executives, powerful trade unions, shady car dealers and even the mafia are part of the compelling cast of characters.

"Wheels" exposes the American car industry and its day-to-day pressures. The plot follows many of the topical issues of the day, including race relations, corporate politics and business ethics. From the grime and crime of a Detroit assembly line to executive boardrooms and bedrooms, Hailey gives us the true heart of motor metropolis, its men and women, their lives, loves and treacheries.

1972 *Watership Down* by Richard Adams

"Watership Down" is set in a quintessential English landscape, but there is an unexpected and deeper meaning to this tale of animal adventures. The rabbits are engaged in a life-or-death struggle against the intrusion of enemies and predators. Although they live in their natural environment, with warrens and burrows, Richard Adams gives them human characteristics and patterns of behaviour.

Each of the rabbits possesses their own unique and interesting identity and such is the power of their friendships and group dynamics that it is difficult not to think of them as people that we like and care about. Armed with great courage and resilience, the rabbits escape the destruction of their warren and establish a new home at Watership Down.

1973 *The Gulag Archipelago* by Aleksandr Solzhenitsyn

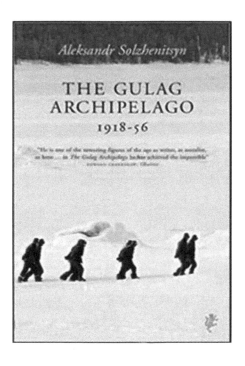

Solzhenitsyn's compelling three volume account of life inside the Soviet Union's prison camps represents the author's attempt to compile a comprehensive account of the state's extensive use of terror against its own population. The unusual title merits a clear explanation of its meaning and importance. Gulag was a Russian acronym for the government agency that was responsible for running the system of labour camps and prisons that housed the political prisoners of the Soviet Union. Also, the title uses the word archipelago as a metaphor for the camps, which were scattered like a chain of islands throughout the country.

Based upon Solzhenitsyn's own eight years of incarceration and the letters and accounts of other prisoners, "The Gulag

Archipelago" is a devastating record of the Soviet regime's brutal atrocities against its own people. After the first volume was published in 1973, the government denounced Solzhenitsyn, leading to his arrest and exile from the country in February 1974.

1974   *The Dogs of War* by Frederick Forsyth

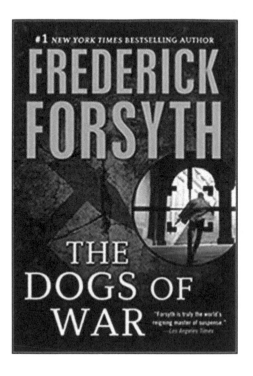

"The Dogs of War", with its title derived from Shakespeare's "Julius Caesar", "Cry, 'Havoc!' and let slip the dogs of war", features a band of European mercenaries hired by a British industrialist to overthrow the government of Zangaro, a fictional country in Africa. In a remote part of the country lies Crystal Mountain, containing enormous deposits of platinum.

The scheming mining tycoon, Sir James Manson, devises a plan to depose the corrupt president and establish a puppet government in order to secure the mining rights to the mountain. For his plan to work, he needs the services of a band of cold-blooded mercenaries. As the action unfolds, Forsyth expertly builds up the tension through detailed descriptions of intricate plans and meticulous preparations.

1975 *Humboldt's Gift* by Saul Bellow

"Humboldt's Gift" is a thinly disguised autobiographical work, with the character of Von Humboldt Fleischer representing the author's friend, the poet and short story writer Delmore Schwartz. Bellow is represented by the narrator of the story, Humboldt's protégé Charlie Citrine. Like Bellow's friend, Humboldt is regarded as a failure and dies ignominiously in relative obscurity.

The problem faced by author and reader alike is that the contrasting careers of the literary figures, both in the novel and in real life, force an examination of what we admire and what we relate to. The extremely talented Humboldt has nothing to show for his work, while Charlie, with less talent, becomes a rich man through his writing. This anomaly is the source of some soul searching about the relationship between artistic and commercial success in the cultural world.

1976   *The Alteration* by Kingsley Amis

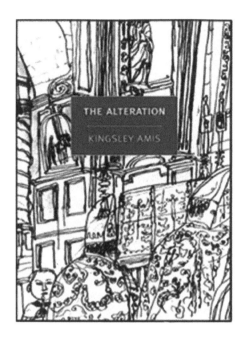

"The Alteration" is an alternative history novel by Kingsley Amis, set in a parallel universe in which the Protestant Reformation never happened. If this invented scenario had actually been real, does Amis think that the world would have been a better place? Many later events such as the Jacobite Rebellion and the French Revolution may have been avoided and the Christian Church would have remained united.

It becomes clear that Amis would not have liked this alternative world, with the Roman Catholic Church holding so much power and intellectual development stagnating. Life would have been more peaceful, but corruption would have been rife. Many readers will feel that they lack the background historical knowledge to fully comprehend the novel, but this should not be the case. "The Alteration" enriches you by taking you to a speculative world that is strange, but somewhat familiar.

1977   *The Shining* by Stephen King

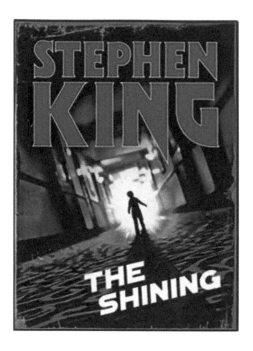

Perhaps better known as a film, due to Jack Nicholson's mesmeric performance, "The Shining" is the classic old fashioned haunted house story. Regarded by many of Stephen King's fans as his finest novel, it centres on the slow progression to madness of Jack Torrance, an aspiring, but alcoholic, writer.

Jack takes his family with him to the historic Overlook Hotel in the Rockies, where he has accepted a position as a caretaker for the winter. Jack's five-year-old son Danny, unknown to his parents, possesses psychic powers, known as "The Shining", that allow him to see the ghosts and frightening visions of the hotel's terrifying past. Being trapped and isolated in the hotel by the Colorado winter, the family are in great danger.

1978 *The Far Pavilions* by MM Kaye

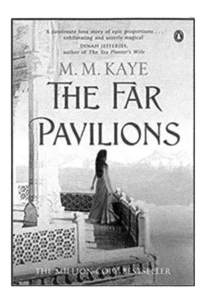

The ultimate novel about 19th century imperial India, "The Far Pavilions" is a captivating journey from beginning to end. Drawing favourable comparisons with Kipling, MM Kaye captures the essence of a very particular time and place with consummate skill. This romantic adventure novel is the story of an English man, brought up as a Hindu after his parents die of cholera, and his passionate, but dangerous love for a beautiful Indian princess.

"The Far Pavilions" is a masterpiece of storytelling in which divided loyalties constantly play on the mind of Ashton Pelham-Martyn and are symbolic of the clash between east and west. The subject matter, like India itself, with its burning plains and snow-capped mountains, is vast, exciting and romantic.

1979 *A Bend in the River* by VS Naipaul
(See Book of the Decade)

The 1980s

Political change arrived at the start of the 1980s, but not perhaps in the way that many people would have expected or hoped for. The dominant politicians of the decade, Ronald Reagan on one side of the Atlantic and Margaret Thatcher on the other, seemed to embody a return to the traditional values of the 1950s, while the "boom and bust" cycle of their free-market economies had more than a feint echo of the 1930s. However, while many people suffered unemployment and economic hardship at the hands of Friedman's economics, many others prospered spectacularly. The growth of technology was inexorable, even if the mobile phones are now viewed as being as laughable as the fashionable shoulder pads of the day.

Both opponents and supporters of the extremely divisive '80s now probably acknowledge that a positive side to the decade was that a growing inter-connectedness was crossing national borders and expanding horizons. Where technology led, perhaps people followed. Perhaps much of today's greater cultural awareness had its birth in this controversial decade.

An era of contrasting views and experiences probably helped the expansion and reception of literature by an even more varied group of writers. The natural extension of post-colonial writing from Africa and Asia was supplemented by European and South American writers adding their names to a much more diverse list of popular literature being consumed in Britain and America. Indeed, works by Italian, Czech, Brazilian and Mexican writers are to be found in our list for the decade.

The 1980s: Book of the Decade

Midnight's Children by Salman Rushdie (1981)

Was post-colonial literature from the late 1970s onwards fixated on India's struggle for independence from Britain? Possibly so, but it did manifest itself in some fantastic fiction. "Midnight's Children" can be described as an allegory for the events on the subcontinent before and after independence and the partition of India and Pakistan. Saleem Sinai, both the protagonist and the narrator of the story, is born at midnight on August 15th 1947; the exact moment when India became an independent country.

Being born at that special time Saleem is a special child. However, this coincidence of birth has consequences that he is not prepared for: telepathic powers connect him with 1,000 other "Midnight's Children", all of whom are endowed with unusual gifts. Inextricably linked to his nation, Saleem's story is a whirlwind of disasters and triumphs that mirrors the course of modern Indian history. He finds himself mysteriously "handcuffed to history" by the coincidences of the period.

"Midnight's Children" is an extraordinary read, but slightly confusing. The vast background of the colours, conflicts and emotions of India are placed at a very particular time, but according to Rushdie himself, "History is always ambiguous" with reality being built on "Prejudices, misconceptions and ignorance as well as on our perceptiveness and knowledge." The glory of this novel is that here literature transcends reality, while simultaneously remaining true to it. "Midnight's Children" is deeply connected to its roots in post-colonial India, but universal in its idea of humanity.

The 1980s: Books of the Year

1980 *The Name of the Rose* by Umberto Eco

Umberto Eco's consummate novel defies any attempts to place it within any narrow genre. A book to be recommended because there's something in it for all tastes. It is so much more than mere historical fiction, murder mystery or thriller. There's theology, philosophy and even some sex to be encountered by the intrepid reader.

Set in 1327 and with the Roman Catholic church in turmoil, Eco brings Brother William of Baskerville to investigate suspected heresy among the Benedictines. Cast as a Medieval Sherlock Holmes, he collects evidence and interprets secret codes, but his mission is overshadowed by a series of mysterious deaths. Murder mystery and religious debate become intertwined as the tensions rise and the plot thickens.

1981 *Midnight's Children* by Salman Rushdie
      (See Book of the Decade)

1982 *The Color Purple* by Alice Walker

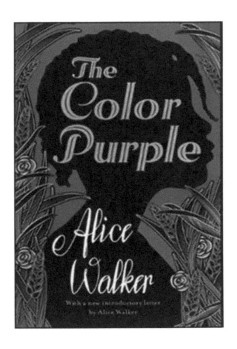

"The Color Purple" is a Pulitzer Prize winning novel that concentrates on the negative experiences of 1930s black women in the southern states of America. The explicit content and high level of violence have meant that Alice Walker's great work has been the frequent target of censors and conservatives alike, but its handling of uncomfortable and controversial subjects has only added to its stature and popularity.

The novel details the life of Celie, a black girl raised in an environment of extreme poverty and racial segregation. However, Alice Walker presents the reader with an inspiring story of one woman's triumphant journey from a life of abuse to one of independence and realisation.

1983   *The Woman in Black* by Susan Hill

"The Woman in Black" is a very atmospheric and spooky read. Although written in the style of a Victorian gothic novel, this story owes much to the 1980s when horror was the dominant genre in both the cinema and the bookshop. Although we feel that we know what should happen next, we may find this story very difficult to put down.

The location is perfect. The creepy Eel Marsh House is dreary and isolated, surrounded by salty marshes and dense fog. The peace of Christmas Eve sees Arthur Kipps alone with the mysterious woman in black, but this peace will be shattered. Can he work out the mystery attached to her and why does she haunt the house?

1984 *The Unbearable Lightness of Being* by Milan Kundera

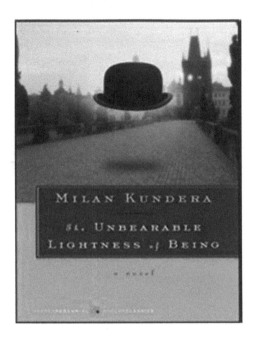

Set mainly in Prague in the late 1960s and early 1970s, "The Unbearable Lightness of Being" examines how the Soviet invasion crushed the artistic, intellectual and political life of Czechoslovakia following the Prague Spring of 1968. As dissent is replaced by repression and truth becomes lost amidst conformity, some of Kundera's characters merge into a background where truth and facts no longer matter.

Against an epic political background, dishonesty abounds in this magnificent story about two desperate couples. Tomas, a successful surgeon, loves Tereza, but cannot resist the charms of other women. Meanwhile, his mistress, the free-spirited artist Sabina is also unfaithful to the intellectual Franz, who earnestly loves her.

1985 *The Handmaid's Tale* by Margaret Atwood

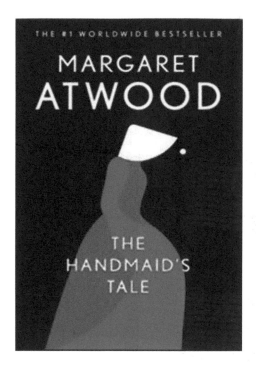

"The Handmaid's Tale", with its name derived from Chaucer's "Canterbury Tales" is a dystopian novel set in the future totalitarian state of Gilead. This feminist tale explores how women are subjugated in a patriarchal society, meaning that Offred, a handmaid, has only one function: that is to breed. If she resists, she will be hanged or sent to die slowly from radiation sickness.

It would appear that Offred has no choices in what is conceived by some people to be a utopian state. Atwood's novel is an unforgettably poignant study of defiance to authoritarian rule that can leave the reader in a state of uncertainty and fear. Offred is broken and desperate, but can she survive?

1986   *The Light Fantastic* by Terry Pratchett

In the delightfully funny "The Light Fantastic" only one person can save the world from a disastrous collision. Unfortunately, the hero happens to be the singularly inept wizard Rincewind, who was last seen falling off the edge of the world. Rincewind meets a series of unbelievable travelling companions as he ambles through a range of unusual and hilarious locations.

However, the real hero of this comic fantasy novel is Pratchett himself. His narration amuses and cajoles us into keeping our concentration. The author is at his most imaginative and fantastical as the characters move from one dangerous and ridiculous situation to another at a rapid pace. Such is the speed of the novel that we almost feel that we are assaulted by the writer's high energy humour.

1987 *Patriot Games* by Tom Clancy

Jack Ryan, a former US Marine is on vacation in London with his pregnant wife and young daughter when he is called upon to thwart a terrorist attack on the Prince of Wales and his family. Jack acts instinctively, never imagining that his intervention could save the lives of Britain's royal family, and is shot. Only afterwards does he realise the importance and implications of his actions.

"Patriot Games" is an extremely realistic and authentic thriller where the focus shifts from its early climatic action to Ryan and his family being the target of extreme Irish terrorists. Jack successfully returns to America with his family. Surely, they must be safe from terrorist retaliation thousands of miles away, or are they?

1988   *The Alchemist* by Paulo Coelho

Paulo Coelho's compelling and enchanting novel details the journey of a shepherd boy named Santiago who travels from his homeland in Spain to the Egyptian pyramids in search of a worldly treasure as glorious as any ever found. He is able to surmount the difficulties he encounters along the way, but his quest is much more than a physical one. Santiago's journey is one of spiritual awareness and awakening.

"The Alchemist" is magical for all those readers whose lives have taken them away from their youthful ambitions and sense of purpose. All the dreams and aspirations that have been forgotten, or have been dismissed as childish fantasy, are reawakened in this book. In reading "The Alchemist" we can both escape reality and understand reality.

1989   *Like Water for Chocolate* by Laura Esquivel

The 1980s closes with another novel that employs magical realism to combine the supernatural with the ordinary throughout its story. "Like Water for Chocolate" is a sumptuous feast of a novel that details the strange history of the all-female De La Garza family. Tita, the youngest daughter of the house, has been forbidden to marry, condemned by Mexican tradition to look after her mother until she dies. However, Tita falls in love with Pedro, and he is seduced by the magical food she cooks. Unfortunately, however, he's married to Tita's sister. Do they have a future?

An international bestseller and an extremely successful film, "Like Water for Chocolate" is a poignant tale worth reading just for the recipes. Perhaps modern TV scheduling has replaced romance with cooking!

The 1990s

What happened in the 1990s? "Not a lot!" would be a many people's answer. Despite not having such strong supporters as the '60s and not being as divisive as the 70s and 80s, this was a decade that saw much change and many climactic events. 1990 alone saw the release of Nelson Mandela from prison, the unification of Germany and the publication of Tim Berners-Lee's formal proposal for the World Wide Web. Life would never be the same again!

A decade of hope gave birth to reconciliation in Northern Ireland and South Africa, but also experienced the genocide of Rwanda and the former Yugoslavia. A reflection of this, and any other decade, may lead us to question that while so much changed, how much was learned? On balance, however, the 1990s has largely been remembered for peace, prosperity and the internet. Britain and America shook off the politics of past ages and found themselves young, vibrant leaders in the form of Tony Blair and Bill Clinton, meaning that both countries viewed the coming millennium with confidence.

Not all was new. The writing of the 1990s had a slightly sentimental feel to it, with "The English Patient", "Birdsong" and "Captain Corelli's Mandolin" all evoking the memories of the 20th century's world wars. What distinguished these great novels, however, was the beauty of the language and the sympathetic portrayal of people placed in extraordinary situations.

The 1990s: Book of the Decade

Birdsong by Sebastian Faulks (1993)

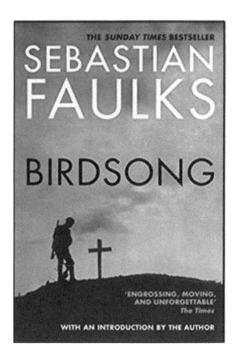

The invented adjective "unputdownable" may have been invented with "Birdsong" in mind. This consummate and compelling novel has such breadth and accuracy that it has been taught in schools and colleges on both the English and history syllabuses. The success of the novel owes much to Faulks' desire to provide an authentic account of what the soldiers of World War I were forced to experience. To this end, he redefined heroism by presenting valour, not in terms of jingoistic patriotism or bravado, but as the endurance of an ever present and pointless suffering.

"Birdsong", however, is much more than a mere war novel. In addition to being a supremely claustrophobic account of life in the tunnels beneath the Western Front, it is a love story where a young Englishman, Stephen Wraysford has a tempestuous love affair with Isabelle Azaire at the house where he stays in France prior to the war. "Birdsong" delivers a moving and shocking account of Stephen's love affair and the trials and hardships of his life as an army officer in the trenches. Such is the power of Faulks' writing that we invariably see life through the eyes of his superbly drawn characters. Although it is not a novel for the faint hearted, "Birdsong" is cleverly and beautifully written. The descriptions of the battlefield are stunningly vivid, making it easy for the reader to visualise the brutality and carnage of life in the trenches.

As Stephen fights for his life in the tunnels, we feel his desperation, we breathe with him and we rejoice at his survival. This novel is great primarily because it portrays the greatness of the human spirit against a background where humanity has almost been destroyed.

The 1990s: Books of the Year

1990 *Amongst Women* by John McGahern

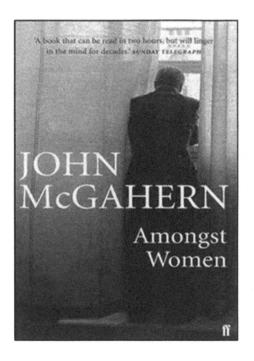

Michael Moran is an old Republican whose life was forever transformed by his days of glory as an early 1920s IRA leader in the struggle for Irish independence. Now, in old age, living out in the country, Moran is still fighting - with his family, his friends, even himself - in a poignant struggle to come to terms with the past.

"Amongst Women" takes its title from the Roman Catholic rosary, where the Virgin Mary is invoked with the words, "blessed art thou amongst women". This is prayed every day in the female dominated Moran household. McGahern's story is one of a strong and violent man facing up to his approaching death surrounded by women who both love him and fear him.

1991   *The Kitchen God's Wife* by Amy Tan

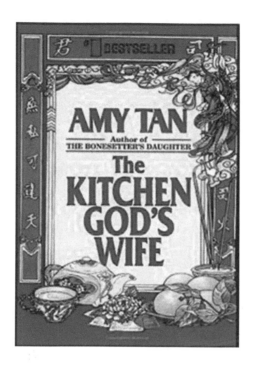

Amy Tan's "The Kitchen God's Wife" deals with Chinese-American female identity and draws on the story of Winnie and Helen, who have kept each other's worst secrets for more than fifty years. Now, because she believes she is dying, Helen wants to expose everything. However, Winnie determines that she must be the one to tell her daughter about the past, including the terrible truth even Helen does not know.

This tour-de-force of a novel takes the reader back to Shanghai in the 1920s, through World War II, to the harrowing events that led to Winnie's arrival in America in 1949. The story is one of innocence and its loss, tragedy and survival and, most of all, the enduring qualities of hope, love and friendship.

1992   *The English Patient* by Michael Ondaatje

With ravishing beauty, Michael Ondaatje's novel traces the intersection of four damaged lives in an Italian villa at the end of World War II: the Canadian Army nurse, the thief, the Sikh bomb disposal expert and the eponymous English patient. All of the other characters are haunted by the riddle of the nameless patient who lies in an upstairs room and whose memories of passion and betrayal illuminate this book like flashes of lightning.

"The English Patient" is a novel of revelation, and just as the identity of the English patient is slowly revealed, so too are the inner selves and spiritual identities of the other characters in the story. It is a beautiful novel that is felt as much as it is read.

1993 *Birdsong* by Sebastian Foulkes
(See Book of the Decade)

1994 *Captain Corelli's Mandolin* by
Louis De Bernières

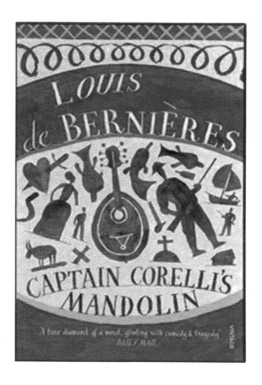

The novel is set on the Greek island of Cephalonia during the Italian and German occupation of Greece in World War II. The officer in command of the Italian garrison is Captain Corelli, whose most precious possession is his mandolin. Love is complicated enough in wartime, even when the lovers are on the same side, but for Corelli and Pelagia, it becomes increasingly difficult to negotiate a minefield of allegiances and relationships.

"Captain Corelli's Mandolin" is a lyrical novel that can take your breath away with its complexity of characters and ideas. Love, if it's real, can survive war. It survives here despite the characters rather than because of them. Like many novels set in wartime, De Bernières' story is a testament to the innate compassion of the human spirit.

1995   *The Horse Whisperer* by Nicholas Evans

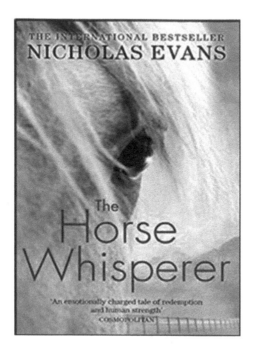

"The Horse Whisperer" is an epic love story with a gripping plot and a magnificent setting. Tom Booker's voice can calm wild horses, his touch can heal broken spirits and Annie Graves has travelled across a continent to the Booker ranch in Montana, desperate to heal her injured daughter, the girl's savage horse and her own wounded heart.

The novel is written beautifully and like many novels that have made it onto the big screen, the book is better than the film. Nicholas Evans creates an extraordinary tale of healing and redemption. It is an emotional journey where the wide Montana landscape creates the perfect backdrop to an exploration of our ancient links with earth and sky.

1996 *Angela's Ashes* by Frank McCourt

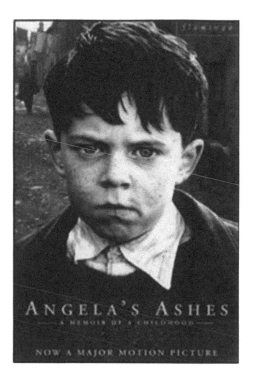

"Angela's Ashes" is an autobiographical memoir about the writer's childhood from his infant years in 1930s Brooklyn tenements, through his adolescence in the slums of Limerick to his return to America at the age of nineteen. It is a story of extreme hardship and suffering, with Frank's mother Angela having to cope with a drunken husband, too many children and not enough money.

With the family constantly being on the brink of disaster, the book is a story of courage and survival against the odds. What is remarkable about Frank McCourt's writing is his distinctive use of humour and an almost unique absence of sentimentality. These qualities put the book firmly in tune with the rich traditions of 20th century Irish writing.

1997 *The God of Small Things* by Arundhati Roy

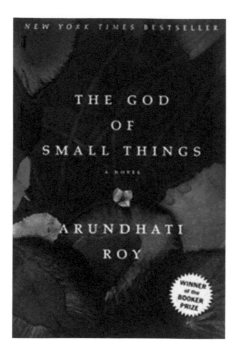

Arundhati Roy's debut novel is set in Kerala in 1969, when twins Rahel and Estha are seven years old, and 23 years later when they return to the family home. Although having achieved independence twenty years earlier, India is still dominated by its caste system. As a result, the early lives and experiences of the twins are destroyed by the "Love Laws" that "lay down who should be loved, and how. And how much."

The book explores how the small things affect people's behaviour and their lives. It is a simple story of a complicated family set against a backdrop of discrimination and bigotry. In this story Arundhati Roy presents a view of an India that is looking to the future, but still hanging on to the traditions of the past.

1998 *About a Boy* by Nick Hornby

Perhaps better known as a 2002 film starring Hugh Grant and Nicholas Hoult, "About a Boy" is a typical Nick Hornby novel in that it is hilarious in a typically English way. Understated and self-effacing humour dominate as the unlikely friendship between the thirty-six-year-old Will and the twelve year-old Marcus develops.

Will is single, cool and has been successful in dating a string of attractive women. One thing that Will is not good at, however, is responsibility. Enter Marcus, the least cool kid ever: the exact opposite of Will. He looks after his mother, listens to classical music and has no awareness of fashion. Marcus needs Will to teach him how to be cool, but Will needs Marcus to help him to grow up.

1999 *Girl with a Pearl Earring* by Tracy Chevalier

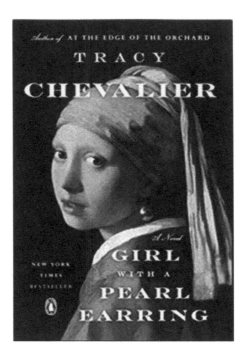

"Girl with a Pearl Earring" is a classic of historical fiction. Set in 17th century Delft, Tracy Chevalier's story was inspired by Dutch painter Johannes Vermeer's famous painting of the same name. The artist's extraordinary paintings of domestic life came to define the Dutch golden age and his depiction of the anonymous "Girl with a Pearl Earring" has been the subject of much conjecture and fascination ever since its creation.

Chevalier mixes history and mystery to produce a supremely absorbing piece of literature. His creation of Griet, Vermeer's maid who is eventually forced to become his model, is extremely well drawn and the narrative is beautifully constructed. The reader becomes involved in a sumptuous story about the relationship between an artist and his subject.

The 2000s

The optimism of a new millennium did not last long. The infamous attack on the Twin Towers on September 11th 2001 led to a sustained "War on Terror", with western political, economic and ideological dominance being threatened in Asia and the Middle East. This decade of turbulence and uncertainty also coincided with a technological revolution which changed the traditional patterns of our lives. Music, film, printed media and the very fabric of our civilisation (books) all came under threat from the gargantuan reach of the internet. Faced with a tsunami of online content, could these traditional means of informing, educating and entertaining people survive?

If the 20th century had been an ongoing battle between ideas, beliefs and ideologies, maybe the 21st century will see victory claimed by the pragmatists. People in the "noughties" began to realise that technology brought choice more than danger to their lives. Everything was changing, but everything remained the same. We still consumed music, film and print, but in a different format. In addition, the Amazon Kindle did not kill the hard copy book. We still like to hold something tangible in our hands and the satisfaction of putting a book down after we have finished reading it remains undiminished.

Added to our choice of format, the writers and their works in this decade was as varied as any other. The historical account, the work of racial consciousness and the post-apocalyptic novel all find a place on our list for the decade.

The 2000s: Book of the Decade

Atonement by Ian McEwan (2001)

Is Ian McEwan Britain's greatest living novelist? To many people, he is and if this is the case, "Atonement" more than any other book is the one that assured him of this title. A gripping and eloquent tale, McEwan's novel is a story that encompasses almost all of human life and experience in their extremes. Set in three distinct time periods: before, during and after World war II, "Atonement" covers love and war, childhood and social class, guilt and forgiveness, but above all, the loss of innocence.

On an idyllic summer's day in 1935, the upper-class Briony Tallis witnesses and then misinterprets events concerning her older sister Cecilia and the son of her father's housemaid,

Robbie Turner. An innocent mistake, allied to an unfettered imagination, by an innocent thirteen-year-old leads to a crime that will have life-changing repercussions for all three characters. It is a mistake that she will spend the rest of her life trying to atone. The presentation of Briony's pivotal scene is beautifully written and sumptuously engaging, but then McEwan displays his whole palette of description with his haunting and sensitive account of a young soldier's struggle to reach home from the battlefields around Dunkirk. If his depiction of character is exquisite, the reader discovers that this is matched by his exploration into the minds of his characters.

Sometimes the subject matter is uncomfortable and disturbing, but we always get a sense that it is portrayed in a way that is appropriate to the plot and the situation. Dramatic as the events in "Atonement" are, they are never sensationalist or gratuitous. It is a true modern classic.

The 2000s: Books of the Year

2000 *White Teeth* by Zadie Smith

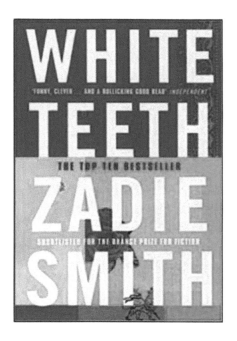

At the centre of "White Teeth" are two unlikely friends, the Bangladeshi Samad Iqbal and the Englishman Archie Jones. Set against London's increasingly diverse racial and ethnic profile, these two veterans of World War II and their families become unwitting agents of what it really means to be classed as British in a multi-cultural society.

Zadie Smith's multi-award-winning novel is both humorous and invigorating as it chronicles the lives of immigrants. The marriages of both Archie and Samad are both funny and complicated in equal measure. Archie's second marriage to Clara, a beautiful Jamaican woman half his age, and Samad's arranged marriage, where he has to wait for his bride to be born, are handled with great dexterity by the writer.

2001 *Atonement* by Ian McEwan
(See Book of the Decade)

2002 *Middlesex* by Jeffrey Eugenides

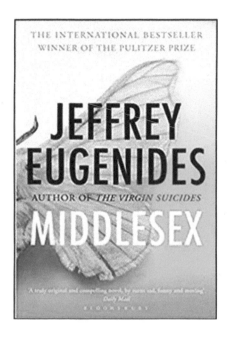

Primarily a coming-of-age story and a family saga, the novel chronicles the effect of a mutated gene on three generations of a Greek-American family, causing momentous changes in the protagonist's life. To understand why Calliope is not like other girls, she has to uncover a guilty family secret and the astonishing genetic history that turns Callie into Cal.

To gain a sense of the plot, but without being told the complete story, the easiest approach is probably to absorb just one quotation from the novel: "I was born twice: first, as a baby girl, on a remarkably smogless Detroit day of January 1960; and then again, as a teenage boy, in an emergency room near Petoskey, Michigan, in August of 1974."

2003   *The Kite Runner* by Khaled Hosseini

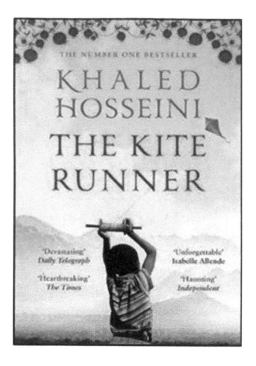

"The Kite Runner" is a wonderfully moving novel set in 1970s Afghanistan which details the story of Amir, a young boy from a wealthy family in Kabul. It is an unforgettable and emotional story of the unlikely friendship between the privileged Amir and Hassan, the son of his father's servant. The two boys are as close as brothers, but the background to their friendship is the tumultuous recent history of a devastated country.

Hosseini's novel is an all-encompassing story of family, love and friendship. The country is in the process of being destroyed and there is a great deal of death and horror in this portrait of a tortured land. However, there is also an emotional richness and a compassionate look into the inner souls of individuals.

2004 *The Plot Against America* by Philip Roth

"The Plot Against America" presents an alternative history in which Franklin D. Roosevelt is defeated in the presidential election of 1940 by Charles Lindbergh the aviation hero and Nazi sympathiser. The major criticism of alternative histories is that the reader requires a knowledge of the actual history. This may have been the case here, but the Trump presidency has served as a great ally to anyone approaching the novel in 2021.

With the celebrity-turned-politician winning the presidency on a platform of fearmongering, latent racism and "America First", the parallels between the isolationist Charles Lindbergh and Donald Trump are unmissable. Against this background, the Jewish-American Roth family of New Jersey find that antisemitism and a lack of tolerance are becoming increasingly accepted in their neighbourhood and their country.

2005 *Never Let Me Go* by Kazuo Ishiguro

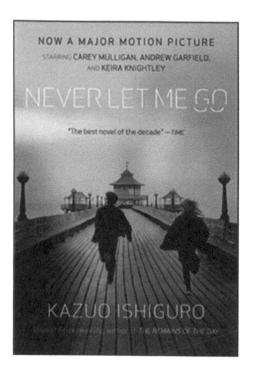

Kazuo Ishiguro's dystopian science fiction novel is a compelling and unforgettable mystery that is heartbreakingly tender and morally courageous about what it means to be human. Within the grounds of Hailsham, an apparently pleasant English boarding school, Kathy grows from schoolgirl to young woman, but it's only when she leaves the safe grounds of the school that she realises the full truth of what Hailsham is.

Far from the influences of the city, Hailsham's students are educated in literature and art to become model citizens. However, curiously and suspiciously, they are taught nothing of the outside world and are allowed only minimal contact with it. As a result, "Never Let Me Go" is both a beautiful love story and a gripping mystery.

2006   *The Road* by Cormac McCarthy

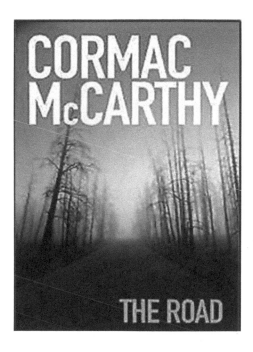

Cormac McCarthy's post-apocalyptic novel details the journey of a father and his young son across an American landscape devastated by an unspecified cataclysmic event that has destroyed almost all of civilisation. Attempting to survive in this brave new world, the young boy and his protector have nothing but a pistol to defend themselves. They must keep walking to the coast to escape the desolate north where only ash remains.

"The Road" is a deeply moving story that imagines a future in which no hope remains, but in which the father and son's love for each other survives. The novel is a gripping appreciation of both the best and the worst that humanity is capable of.

2007   *The Girl Who Kicked the Hornet's Nest*
by Stieg Larsson

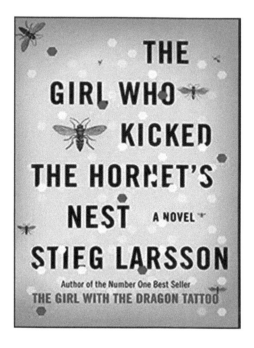

Following on from "The Girl with the Dragon Tattoo" and "The Girl Who Played with Fire", "The Girl Who Kicked the Hornet's Nest" is the stunning third novel in Stieg Larsson's internationally best-selling "Millennium" series. Such has been the impact of Larsson's writing that all three novels have been made into successful films.

Lisbeth lies in a critical condition from a bullet wound to her head in the intensive care unit of a Swedish hospital. She has to fight for her life in more ways than one: if she recovers, she will be taken back to Stockholm to stand trial for three murders. She will not only have to prove her innocence, but also identify those in authority who have allowed her to suffer such violence.

2008 *The White Tiger* by Aravind Adiga

Aravind Adiga paints an unflattering portrait of India as a class-ridden and corrupt society in this darkly humorous novel. Balram Halwai is "The White Tiger"- the smartest boy in his village. Unfortunately, his family is too poor to afford for him to finish school and he is forced to work in a teashop, breaking coals and wiping tables. However, he gets a lucky break when a rich man hires him as a chauffeur and takes him to live in Delhi.

India's capital, with all its shops and riches proves to be a revelation to him. This is a city of opportunity, but his opportunities are limited. How can he enter this world of wealth and privilege? Perhaps by murdering his landlord!

2009 *Wolf Hall* by Hilary Mantel

Regarded by most critics as one of the greatest historical novels of all time, Hilary Mantel's work is named after the family seat in Wiltshire of Jane Seymour, third wife of Henry VIII. "Wolf Hall" is a powerful fictionalised biography which documents Thomas Cromwell's inexorable rise to power within the Tudor court.

In this dramatic work, set in 1520s England, the country is on the brink of disaster. If the king dies without a male heir, the country could lurch into civil war. Henry VIII wants to annul his marriage of twenty years to Catherine of Aragon and marry Anne Boleyn, but the Pope, the Catholic Church and most of Europe are against him. Into this impasse steps the cunning and opportunist Thomas Cromwell whose personal ambitions are almost limitless.

The 2010s

The decade opened in April 2010 with the launch of the iPad; a symbol if ever one was needed, that technology was not only marching on, but becoming increasingly affordable for the vast majority of people in the west. It could be argued that as technology advanced, ideas went backwards. Some things, it appears, never change and the 2010s saw the regular generational lurch to the political right that took place every thirty years throughout the twentieth century. Just as the political landscape of the 1980s mirrored the conservatism of the 1950s, so the 2010s saw a Conservative government in power in the UK throughout the decade and Donald Trump's domination of the political stage from 2016 onwards.

As the power of social media expanded, so the boundaries of what was reality and what was "Fake News" became increasingly blurred. In an era when discerning the truth became a creative activity, it should not surprise us that the creative minds of writers turned their focus back to the reliable plots and settings of yesteryear for clarity. Richard Flanagan's "The Narrow Road to the Deep North" used the haunting memories of World War Two as his backdrop, "My Brilliant Friend" was set in a poor immigrant neighbourhood and "The Nickel Boys" returned to the subject matter of 1960s civil rights.

The 2010s: Book of the Decade

Milkman by Anna Burns (2018)

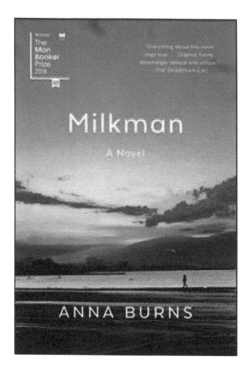

Set during the Northern Ireland "Troubles" of the 1970s, the story follows an 18-year-old girl who is harassed by an older married man known as the "Milkman". As well as having to avoid the unwanted attentions of a creepy, psychopathic paramilitary, the narrator recounts her teenage experiences of trying to steer a path through the minefield of political intrigue and secretive gossip on the Catholic side of a divided community.

At the heart of the novel is the trapped young female whose only escape from this grim existence is her love of literature. To add to the atmosphere of extreme secrecy, Anna Burns places the unnamed teenager in an unnamed city populated by equally anonymous citizens. A further layer of intrigue is created by this innovative method of not using names, but instead referencing the characters by their place within the plot. Hence, the "Milkman", who stalks the "middle sister" is also a "renouncer of the state".

Not only are characters referred to in the most indirect of ways, so too are the locations and communities. The "interface roads" and the "ten-minute area" add to the level of menace that the protagonist regularly encounters. Her love of books and literature, rather than politics and religion, mark her out as a suspicious character within her family and her community. People with independent opinions attract interest and to be noticed is extremely dangerous. She manages to keep her head down, quite literally, by burying it in a book while she walks. Her observation that, "This would be a 19th-century book because I did not like the 20th-century," is an extremely perceptive one.

The 2010s: Books of the Year

2010   *A Visit from the Goon Squad* by Jennifer Egan

"A Visit from the Goon Squad" contains a bewildering combination of thirteen interrelated narratives which all revolve around Bennie Salazar and his assistant, Sasha. Bennie is an aging punk rocker and record executive, while Sasha is a passionate and troubled young woman.

The complex set of stories is accompanied by an extremely large set of mostly self-destructive characters, who, as they grow older, are taken in unforeseen, and sometimes unusual, directions by life. The multitude of stories move backward and forward in both time and location. This complex novel moves from the 1970s to the present day and into the near future. Many of the stories take place in and around New York City, but other settings include San Francisco, Italy, and Kenya.

2011 *The Sense of an Ending* by Julian Barnes

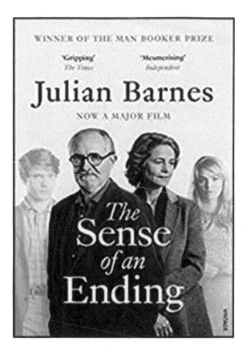

Julian Barnes' novel follows a middle-aged man as he contends with a past that he has never thought much about - until his closest childhood friends return with a vengeance. Tony Webster has built a life for himself, but he is then presented with a mysterious legacy that obliges him to reconsider a whole variety of things that he thought he'd understood all along and to revise his estimation of his own nature and place in the world.

Written by an author of consummate skill and understated brilliance, "The Sense of an Ending" is the story of an ordinary and respectable man coming to terms with his seemingly unremarkable past. A relatively short novel with few, if any, wasted words, Barnes' unforgettable story has been read by many people at a single sitting.

2012 *My Brilliant Friend* by Elena Ferrante

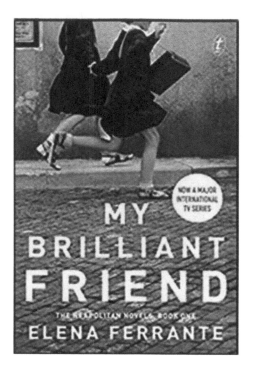

A modern masterpiece, "My Brilliant Friend" is a rich, intense and heart-warming story about two friends, Elena and Lila. As the opening novel of Ferrante's much acclaimed "Neapolitan Quartet", it is both the story of a nation and a touching meditation on the nature of friendship. Growing up on the tough streets of a poor 1950s Italian neighbourhood, the two girls learn to rely on each other and as they grow, their paths repeatedly diverge and converge.

Many acclaimed novels fail to live up to their reputations, but "My Brilliant Friend" deserves all the praise that has been heaped upon it. This is a book that captures a particular time and place with complete authority, while portraying its two main characters with both compassion and depth.

2013 *The Goldfinch* by Donna Tartt

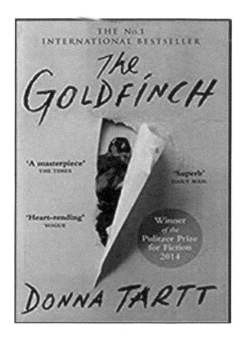

Containing nearly eight hundred pages, "The Goldfinch" has been criticised for being unnecessarily long. However, much of the intensely descriptive detail is both necessary and fascinating. Donna Tartt's coming-of-age novel is an intense and insightful study of loss and belonging. With action on every page and memorable characters created, it can be described as an enthralling psychological thriller.

"The Goldfinch" is a coming-of-age novel in which the protagonist, 13-year-old Theodore Decker, survives a terrorist bombing at New York's Metropolitan Museum. Unfortunately, his mother is killed in the explosion. Struggling alone among the debris, Theo picks up a small painting called "The Goldfinch" by Carel Fabritius, a student of Rembrandt. Somehow, he never finds the courage to return the work to its rightful owners and thus begins his descent into crime.

2014 *The Narrow Road to the Deep North* by **Richard Flanagan**

"The Narrow Road to the Deep North" is an epic novel which covers the cruelty of war, the impossibility of love and the extreme fragility of life. An Australian doctor, Dorrigo Evans has become something of a celebrity in old age, as a result of the public's interest in him as a war veteran.

However, he is haunted by memories of an illicit affair with his uncle's wife and of his experiences as a prisoner of the Japanese during the construction of the Burma Railway. Decades later, he is plagued by his own shortcomings and his feelings of failure and guilt. At the heart of the story is a single day in August 1943 where Dorrigo fails in his attempt to save the lives of some of his fellow prisoners.

2015 *The Girl on the Train* by Paula Hawkins

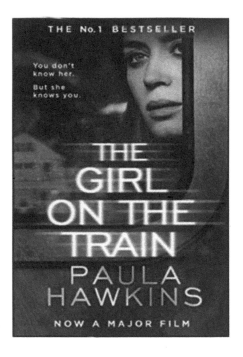

Paula Hawkins' novel is a tightly woven mystery story which reveals some startling truths and painful secrets along the way. The major character, Rachel Watkins, is at an extremely vulnerable stage of her life. Drinking too much and having lost both her job and her husband, she continues to catch the same commuter train into the city, just as she did when she was in work.

Rachel knows that the train will wait at the same signal every day, overlooking a row of back gardens. Observing life through the window, she begins to feel that she knows the inhabitants of one of the houses. Creating a story about a couple, whose life appears to be perfect, only serves to make Rachel envious, but then she witnesses something to shatter all her illusions.

2016 *Another Brooklyn* by Jacqueline Woodson

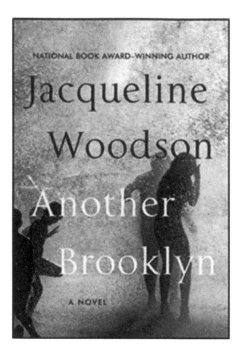

The story starts with August returning to Brooklyn following the death of her father. On the subway ride back to clean her father's apartment, she meets Sylvia, someone she was close friends with as a child and begins to reminisce about her childhood in the summer of 1973.

The novel then follows August through her teenage years, where she and her inseparable friends shared optimistic dreams of the future. Brooklyn was a place where they belonged and believed that they had a brilliant future. However, the reality of her neighbourhood was somewhat different. Beneath the hopeful exterior lay another Brooklyn, a dark and perilous place of crime and danger. This is a novel where childhood, in which friendship was everything, gives way to adulthood, where innocence is just a memory.

2017 *Sing, Unburied, Sing* by Jesmyn Ward

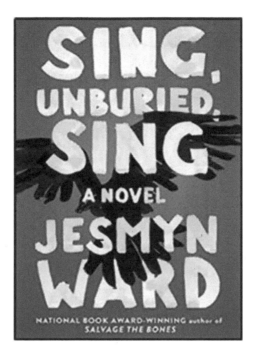

"Sing, Unburied, Sing" is a haunting novel that portrays the difficulties of a single family as they struggle against the odds in coastal Mississippi. Alongside the struggle there is hope, but the ugly truths of a racially divided country are what last longest in the reader's consciousness.

Jojo is a thirteen-year-old boy forced to grow up too quickly, while his mother, Leonie, has not grown up enough to help her children. She desperately wants to be a better mother, but the odds are stacked against her. She is black and her children's father is white. However, her biggest conflict is with herself. She cares about her children, but she is unable to put them before her own needs, particularly her reliance on drugs.

2018 *Milkman* by Anna Burns

(See Book of the Decade)

2019 *The Nickel Boys* by Colson Whitehead

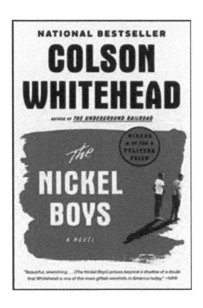

As the American Civil Rights movement reaches the black quarter of racially segregated Tallahassee, Elwood Curtis is caught up by the passions and ideals of Martin Luther King's rhetoric. Believing in emancipation and equality, he is excited about his imminent enrolment at a local black college. However, for a black boy in the early 1960s, one innocent slip is enough to destroy his future.

When Elwood is unfairly sentenced to a juvenile reformatory called the Nickel Academy, he finds himself trapped in a grotesque world of racism, sexual abuse and torturous brutality. This is a coming-of-age story, where growing up is distorted by the atrocities witnessed and experienced. Ironically, the more he understands about freedom, the less freedom he is given.

And finally....

2020 *Apeirogon* by Colum McCann

What is the meaning of "Apeirogon"? Mathematically it is a polygon with a countably infinite number of sides. Life has many sides and an infinite number of possibilities. It can be a puzzle, but it should never be viewed as one dimensional. What Colum McCann's novel explores is a complex relationship between two bereaved men: one an Israeli and the other a Palestinian. Within this world of conflict, we are invited to respect both men, but to side with neither.

Both men's daughters are killed in a conflict that influences all aspects of life in this disputed land. Unusually, the two men become friends and as befits a novel that is named after a multi-sided shape, "Apeirogon" has many facets. It is a skilful exploration of friendship, loss, and identity.

The Present and the Future

If we are exhausted from reading a range of novels interrupted by the odd autobiography, perhaps we can reflect upon the words of one the great poets:

Time present and time past
Are both perhaps present in time future,
And time future contained in time past.
If all time is eternally present
All time is unredeemable.
What might have been is an abstraction
Remaining a perpetual possibility
Only in a world of speculation.
What might have been and what has been
Point to one end, which is always present.
Footfalls echo in the memory
Down the passage which we did not take
Towards the door we never opened
Into the rose-garden.

"Four Quartets 1: Burnt Norton" by TS Eliot

So, our century of reading that began in a pandemic, ends in the same way. "Time past" and "time present" are uncannily similar. We look forward with optimism towards the future, much as our ancestors in the 1920s did. The final novel on the list covers a conflict that seems to have always been with us. Will there ever be a workable solution, or is mankind destined to live in a world of division? Has our recent lockdown world given us the opportunity to think about creating a fairer world?

As we venture out, we must open "the door we never opened into the rose-garden" of a beautiful new world. The literary wisdom of Eliot, unparalleled since the time of Shakespeare, tells us that "All time is unredeemable." There is much to learn and much to read.